PRIGS
Seven Virtuous Lady
GARDENERS
ENGRAVINGS BY EDWINA ELLIS
VERSE BY CAROLINE PALMER

Smith
Settle

First published in 1997 by
Smith Settle Ltd
Ilkley Road
Otley
West Yorkshire
LS21 3JP

Engravings © Edwina Ellis 1997
Text © Caroline Palmer 1997

Editor Penny David

ISBN 1 85825 076 5

British Library Cataloguing-in-Publication data:
A catalogue record for this book is available from the British
Library.

Designed, printed and bound by
SMITH SETTLE
Ilkley Road, Otley, West Yorkshire LS21 3JP

Faith

Hope

Charity

Prudence

Temperance

Justice

Fortitude

The Seeds of Serendipity

First there were Edwina Ellis' prints. They germinated as a light-hearted consideration of the Virtues as gardeners, and developed into garden products with those names (with the exception of Temperance, who recycled a Parsimony packet to store her dandelion roots) — flowering in the series of colour engravings *Seven Products of Virtue as Garden Prigs*.

Uprooted from the rich soil of Kensington and transplanted to the isolation of a remote cottage in west Wales, Edwina found herself eagerly awaiting Wednesdays for the appearance of the *Cambrian News*. There, shining like a friendly beacon among accounts of sheep-subsidies, speeding fines, high winds and low-flying jets she found one luminous column — Caroline Palmer's weekly horticultural excursion in prose.

Artist and author found common ground in the back of a bus, as fellow members of Cardiganshire Horticultural Society outings, and the idea arose that Caroline should write some text to accompany Edwina's already well-loved colour engravings.

As Caroline contemplated the multi-layered content of the prints they seemed to speak for themselves: attempts at wordy essays on virtuous themes merely shrivelled. Eventually she laid her prose pen aside and took up the pronged instrument of verse. Faith, Prudence and the sisterhood romped into rhyme. More chuckles were heard from the back of the bus as ***Prigs*** the book thrust confident leaves to the light.

You need much more than simple faith
To garden well at Dyffryn Paith.
Faith learned too late, to her dismay,
The builders took the soil away
And spread it out upon the land
On which the council chambers stand.

At Dyffryn Paith the agent's blurb
Omits fat hen and willowherb
Bright fumitory, creeping moss
The Council's gain is gardeners' loss.

But Faith buys topsoil, peat and sand
And gets her garden built as planned
With borders, rocks and butyl pond
An instant garden smoothly lawn'd.
She buys in turf, the plants, the seed,
She didn't bargain for knotweed.

The inconspicuous chunky nodes
Throughout the topsoil brought in loads
Awoke next spring with fleshy shoots
And soon extended wrist-thick roots
Through turf and rockery, lawn and dell—
They punctured through the pool as well.

Faith is not daunted, Faith can wait

She's drenched the place in glyphosate

And while the garden's drear and bare

She plants an acorn here and there

For Faith endures, and Faith does know

Great oaks from little acorns grow.

Wishful thinking cannot hurt you —
Hope's not silly, hope's a virtue.
Hope is dogged, always trying
To grow those plants it's not worth buying.

The limey soil will not deter
Her choice of Rhodos, Noble Fir
Camellias, blue Lithodora
Nurserymen wait keenly for her.
Back she comes to buy new stock
How *can* there be pH in rock?

The winter catalogues of seeds
Fulfil her fantasies and needs
For Shirley Poppies, Rhodochiton,
No propagation hints to frighten
Purchasers, until the pack
Arrives, instructions on the back,
Demanding glass, brown paper, heat —
Stringent requirements she must meet.
She buys a heated propagator,
Greenhouse with thermo-ventilator,
Then finds the year has slipped away,
She's failed to plant from March to May.

Hope's aspirations never pale,
Though half her schemes are doomed to fail.
She hankers after all that's new
And loathes her sister's box and yew
Whose home, instead of urns of plastic,
Boasts arches and chessmen, birds fantastic.
Through topiary can Hope's relation,
Patience, proclaim her social station.

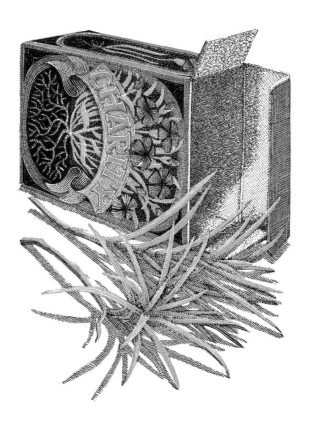

When you open to the public
They come along and say
'Oh what a lovely shrub that is'
And take a piece away.

They also like to know the names
Of all the plants on view.
They never bring a notebook
So they take the labels too.

They like a pretty garden
And expect a damn good tea,
And although it's all for charity
Take extra cakes for free.

Because they weren't invited
Inside the house to pass,
You'll find them in the flowerbeds
Their faces to the glass.

They believe that in the Garden Scheme
You're in a well-heeled club
With your name at Lloyds of London
And security by Chubb.

When cats beneath the window scratch
Or nesting birds invade the thatch
When slugs infest the cabbage patch
They'll rarely find themselves a match
      For Prudence of Shallot.
As with her arsenal of potions
Pellets, scarecrows, nets and lotions
Prudence sets aside emotions
      To defend her plot.

The birds recoil at silhouettes
Of cats among the onion sets
The raspberries ripen under nets
A Webley pistol settles debts
      For Pru's a deadly shot.

A good supply of pepper-dust
Distracts the cats' nocturnal lust
Good gardening means that Prudence must
          Keep creatures off her plot.

But summer's long, and warm and dry
And underneath her watchful eye
Alights a pretty butterfly
Whose caterpillars swiftly try
          To gobble up the lot.
While safe from cats, the busy voles
Are dragging raspberries down their holes
Until the canes stand bare as poles
          In Pru's protected spot.

Pru by the hearthside bright with rugs
Once more surveys the catalogues
To deal with aphids, mealy bugs
New Zealand flatworm, snails and slugs
                    The canker and blackspot.

She'll combat by anticipation
Every threat to cultivation,
Riled by nature's provocation
                    She'll suppress a lot.

Temperance will not invest
In every plant that's new or best
She hoards her seed,
Divides the hostas,
While Hope sunbathes on the Costas
Temperance dispels the gloom
With wintersweet to scent the room.

She has no planned designer features
Terrace, pool, or sculpted creatures
Her towering Delphs
And Banksian roses
Forget-me-nots and tuberoses
All descend direct from plants
Belonging to her maiden aunts.

Temperance always gardened thus
No waste, few poisons, little fuss,
But suddenly
She finds she's queen
Of a new movement labelled 'Green'.

Her books provide the means by which
Our parsimony makes her rich.
She shows us how to make herb tea
From acorns or agrimony,
While dandelions (the roasted root)
Make splendid coffee substitute.

I've heard it said, 'It is sublime
To let the punishment fit the crime'.
It's not enough to poison bugs
Or sharply stamp on snails and slugs.

These days justice is much rougher
Science breakthroughs make them suffer
And embryo threadworms sent by mail
Will eat their way through slug or snail
Till after weeks of hunchbacked toil
The slug explodes, a worm-filled boil.

Though Justice had an interest vested

In a garden that's infested

With these patent parasites,

Their lifestyle gave her sleepless nights.

Feeling nauseous, Justice tried

To kill them with metaldehyde.

But anxious for her frogs and hedgehogs

Laid out planks of seasoned elm logs,

These she lifted every day

And gently took her catch away.

Traps with beer, or jars of brine

Are favourite remedies of mine.

For pogrom swift, out of the blue,

Take scissors, snip each slug in two.

The Aga's cold, the bird bath froze
Edwina wonders why she chose
To garden on this windswept slope
Eschewed by Prudence, scorned by Hope,
While the phlegm drips down her nose.

The ground is clay bound hard with ice
The corms and bulbs sustain the mice
The Albertine's blown off the shed
The Pieris and the Acer dead.
But the summer views were nice.

The septic tank has overflowed
And frozen sewage skins the road.
She's made a desperate proposal
To Plynlimon Waste Disposal.
But they don't work when it's cold.

The trellis flaps. The beech trees roar.
Her head and throat are getting sore.
But February's just the middle
Of the West Wales country idyll.
June will come once more.

About the Authors

Engraver Edwina Ellis prodded (with a fork and spoon) a row of pots upon a London balcony for twenty years, and felt experienced enough to dig at gardeners in her series of prints *Seven Products of Virtue as Garden Prigs*. As she set about personifying the Virtues as gardeners, they — and the Virtues themselves for that matter — seemed less and less virtuous. Ensconced in West Wales since 1992 (and now digging a proper garden), she continues to work with three engraved blocks to create her unique and sought-after full-colour prints.

Author Caroline Palmer combined writing light verse with her former career in anthropology at Oxford University. Since migrating to Aberystwyth in 1982, she has turned her forked pen to a scrutiny of local gardening mores for her acclaimed 'Garden Gossip' column in the *Cambrian News*, and her book *Cuttings – a Gardeners' pot pourri from Wales* (Gomer Press, 1996). Invariably as fascinated by the gardener as by the garden, she rose eagerly to the challenge of depicting seven virtuous lady gardeners in verse.

Limited edition original prints of the *Prigs* by Edwina Ellis, singly or in a boxed set, are available from Smith Settle publishers.

For further details of these, and our other publications, contact

Ilkley Road
Otley
West Yorkshire

LS21 3JP